Trace and Color

Go with the flow, follow the lines and enter a zen like state of relaxation. Trace and Color: Christmas Trees lets you recreate 40 adorable Christmas Trees using nothing more than a pen or pencil. Each page in this book features a detailed drawing printed in a light gray color. All you have to do is follow the lines, relax and watch the time slip away.

Once you are finished tracing the image, you can add as little or as much color as you want. It is like having two books in one.

"I came up with the idea for Trace and Color when I was drawing up pages for an adult coloring book. I noticed how time seemed to slip away and I forgot about all my troubles. Being able to give you the same opportunity to relax and unwind is a true blessing. Just follow the lines and watch the time slip right on by!"

Thank you for purchasing a copy of my book. I had a great time creating this book for you and I would to see what you do with the designs. Feel free to email me images of what you have colored. My email address is:

bethingrias@gmail.com

If you enjoyed coloring my designs, then please leave a review to let others know what you thought, be it good or bad. Leaving a review is the single best way to help support me and my art. Leaving a review is easy and don't forget to post a completed colored page with your review.

FREE BONUS!

Get 25 FREE coloring pages at my website.

www.bethingrias.com

ISBN-13: 978-1-945803-36-9
ISBN-10: 1-945803-36-3

Tracing Tips

Place a piece of paper or thick card stock under each page before tracing. This will help prevent your tracing lines from appearing on other pages in the book.

Use a fine tipped pencil at first. This way you can erase your happy accidents.

Ball point pens glide easily across the pages.

Try tracing with a colored pencil for a truly unique, artistic effect.

Fine tipped charcoal or graphite works great too. You can even use either of these to hone your shading techniques.

Oh yeah, Have lots of fun!

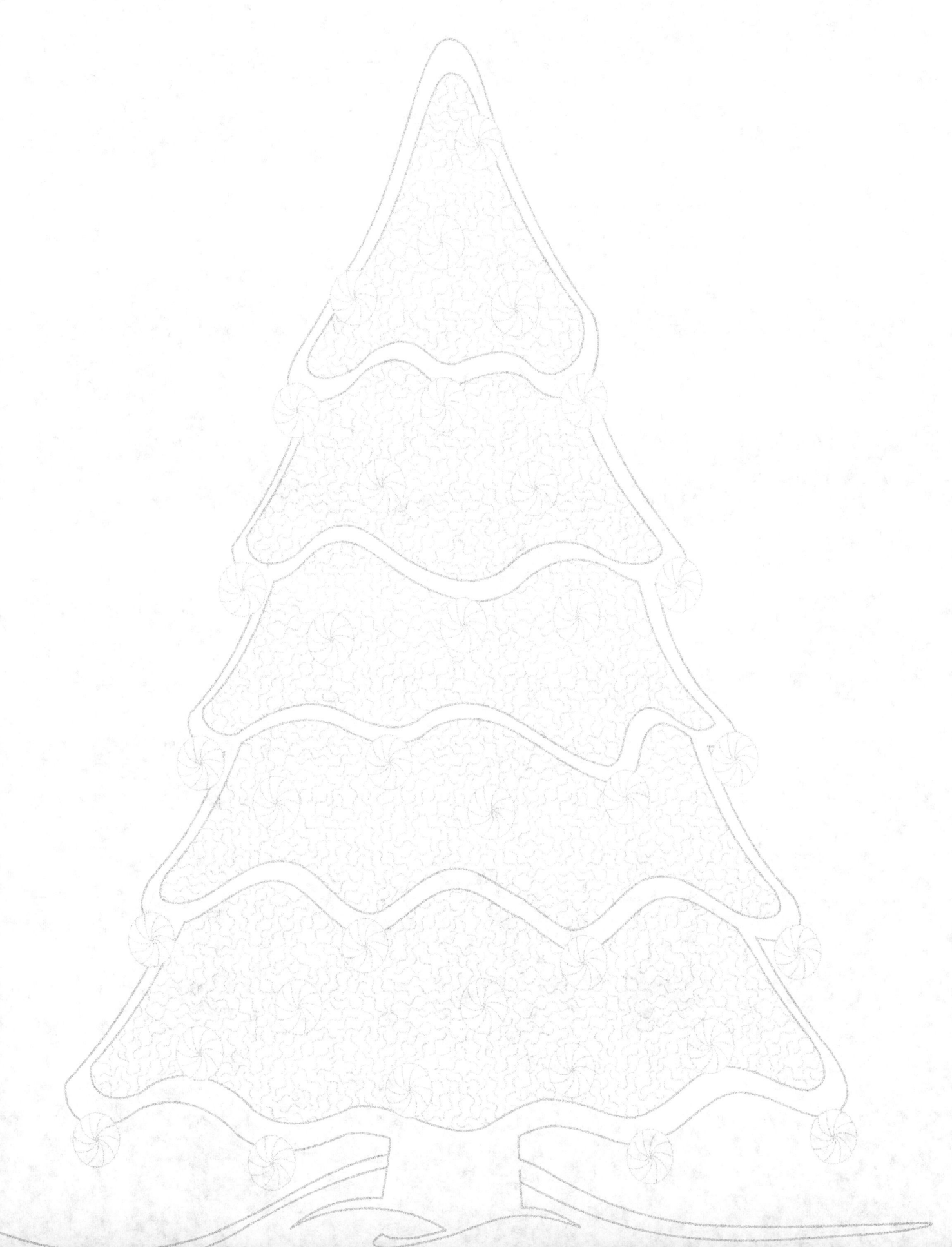

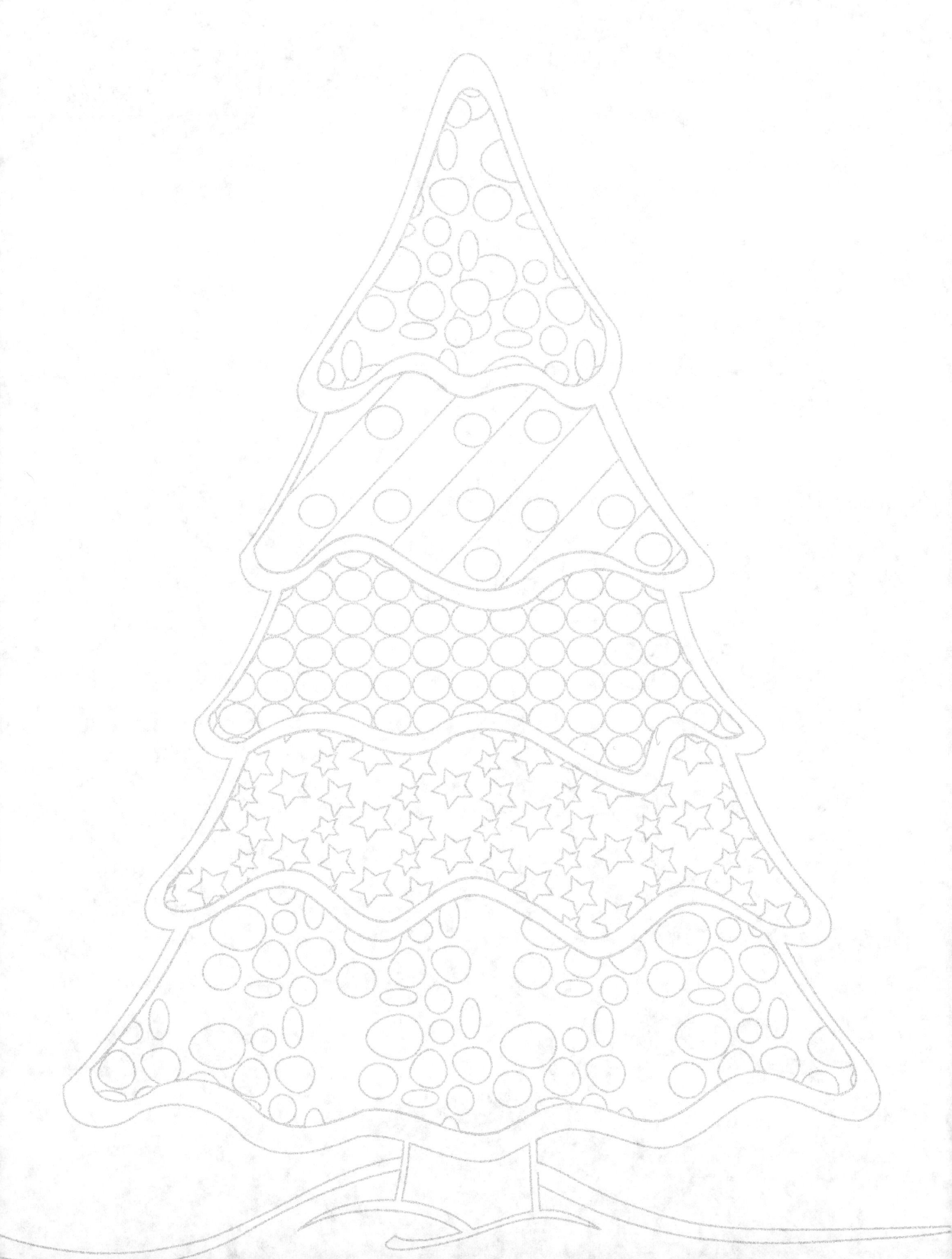

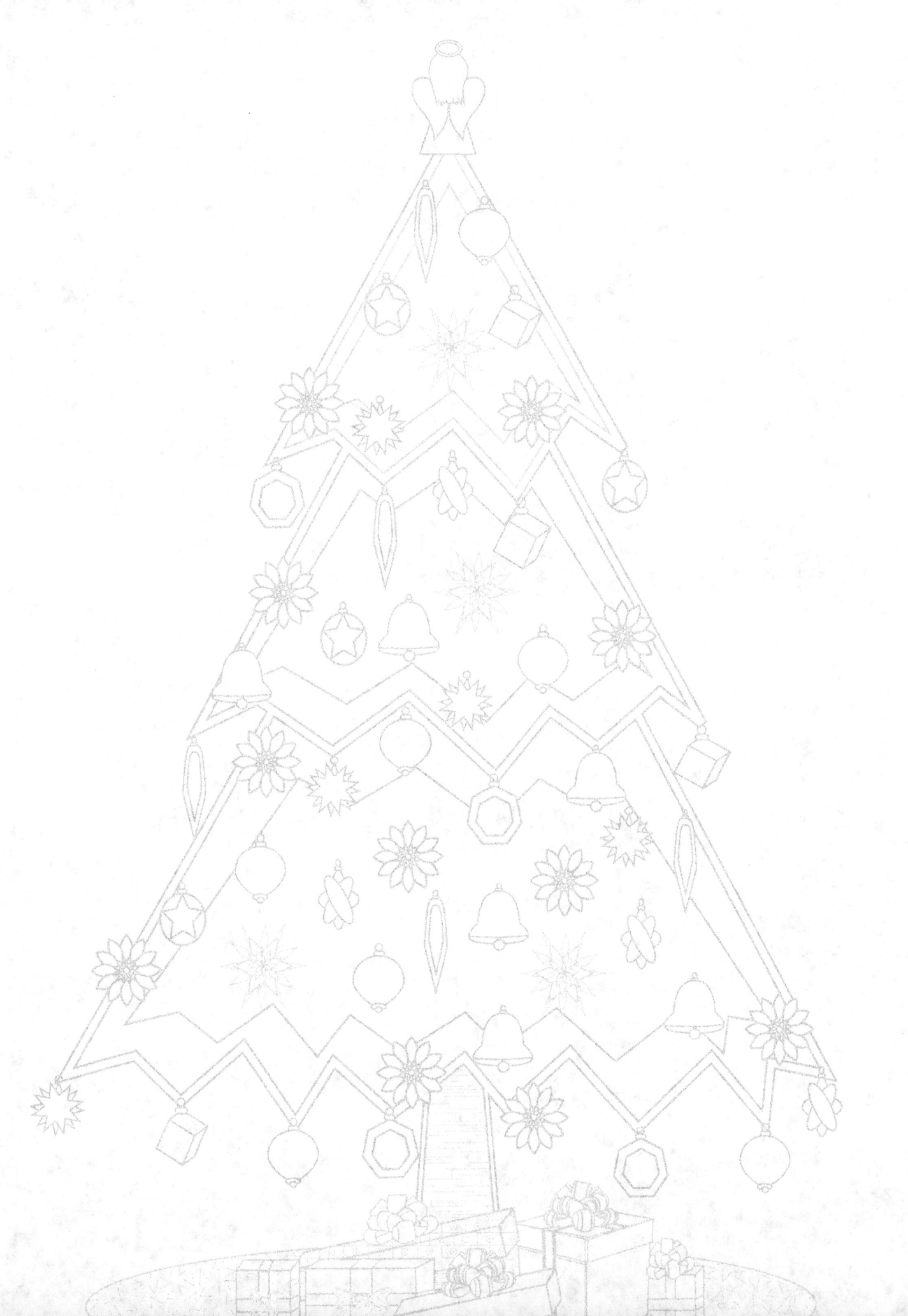

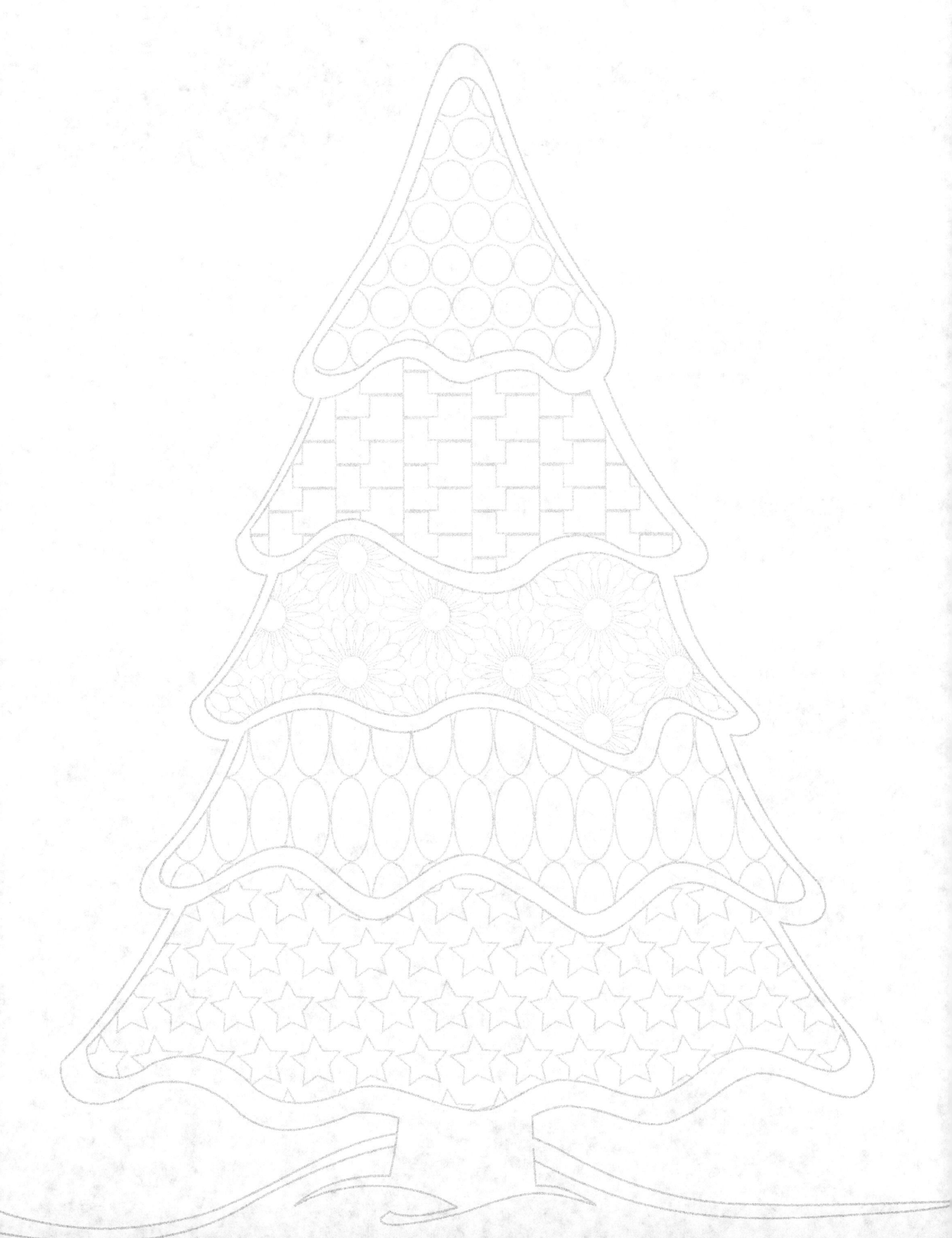

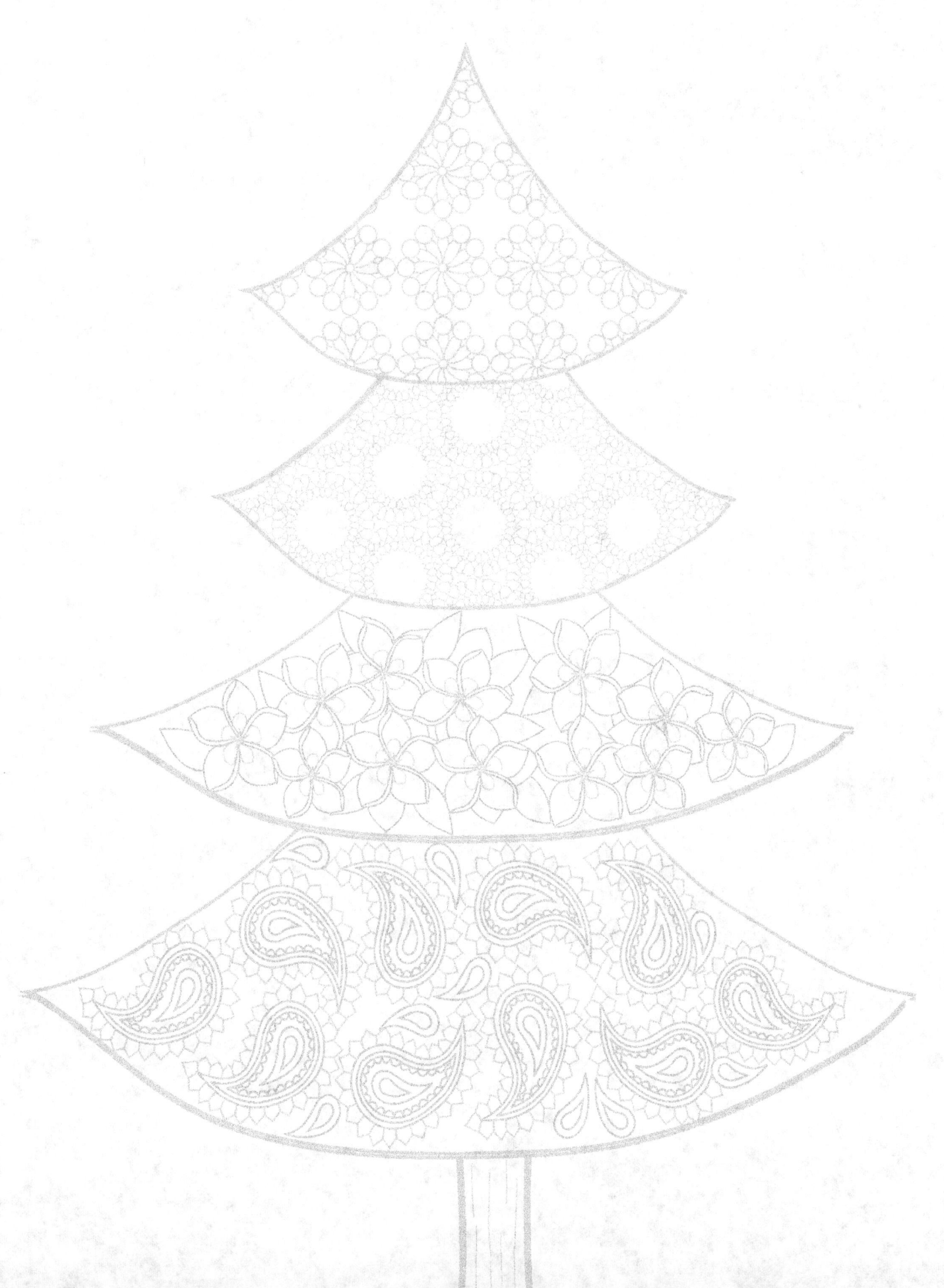

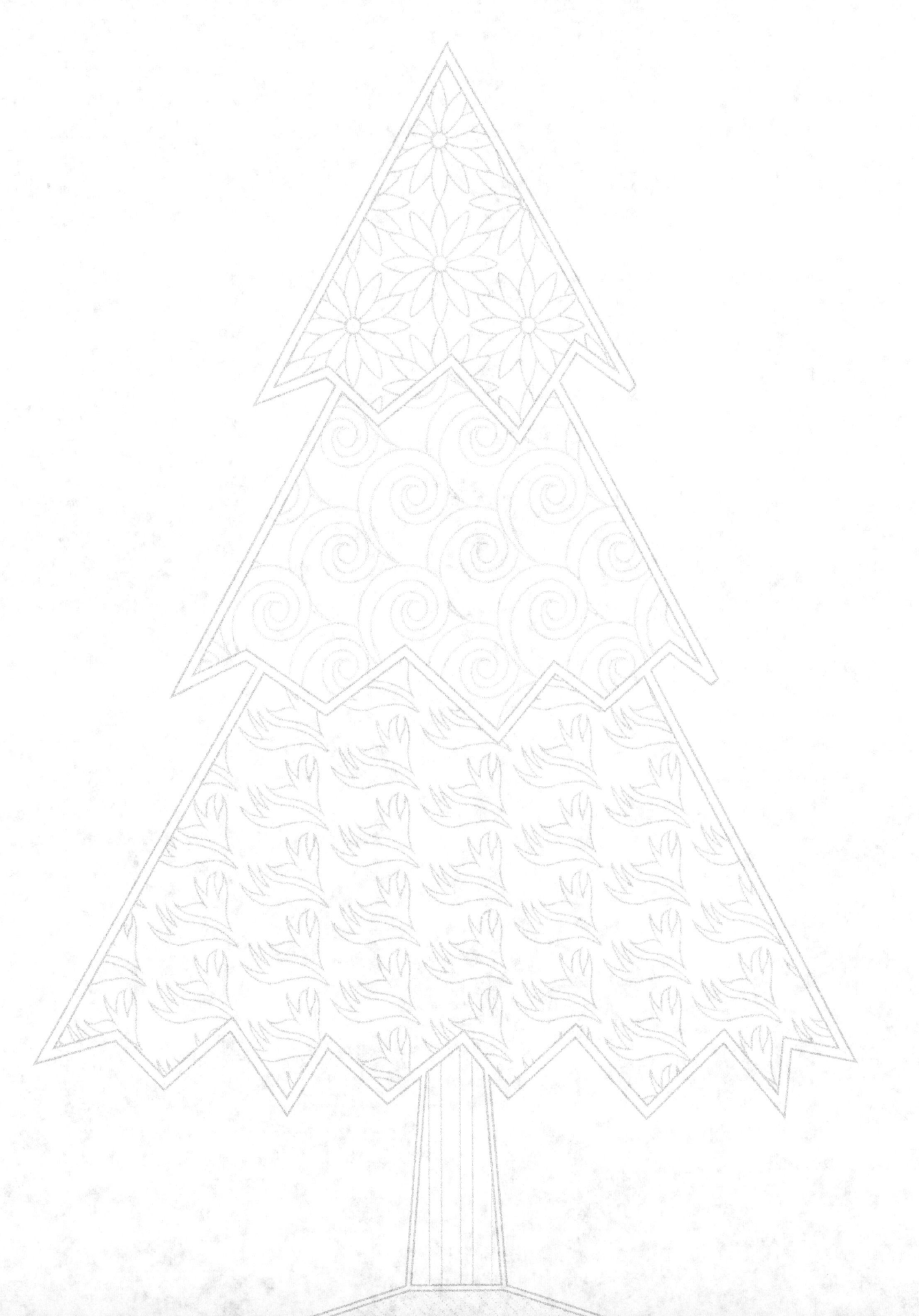

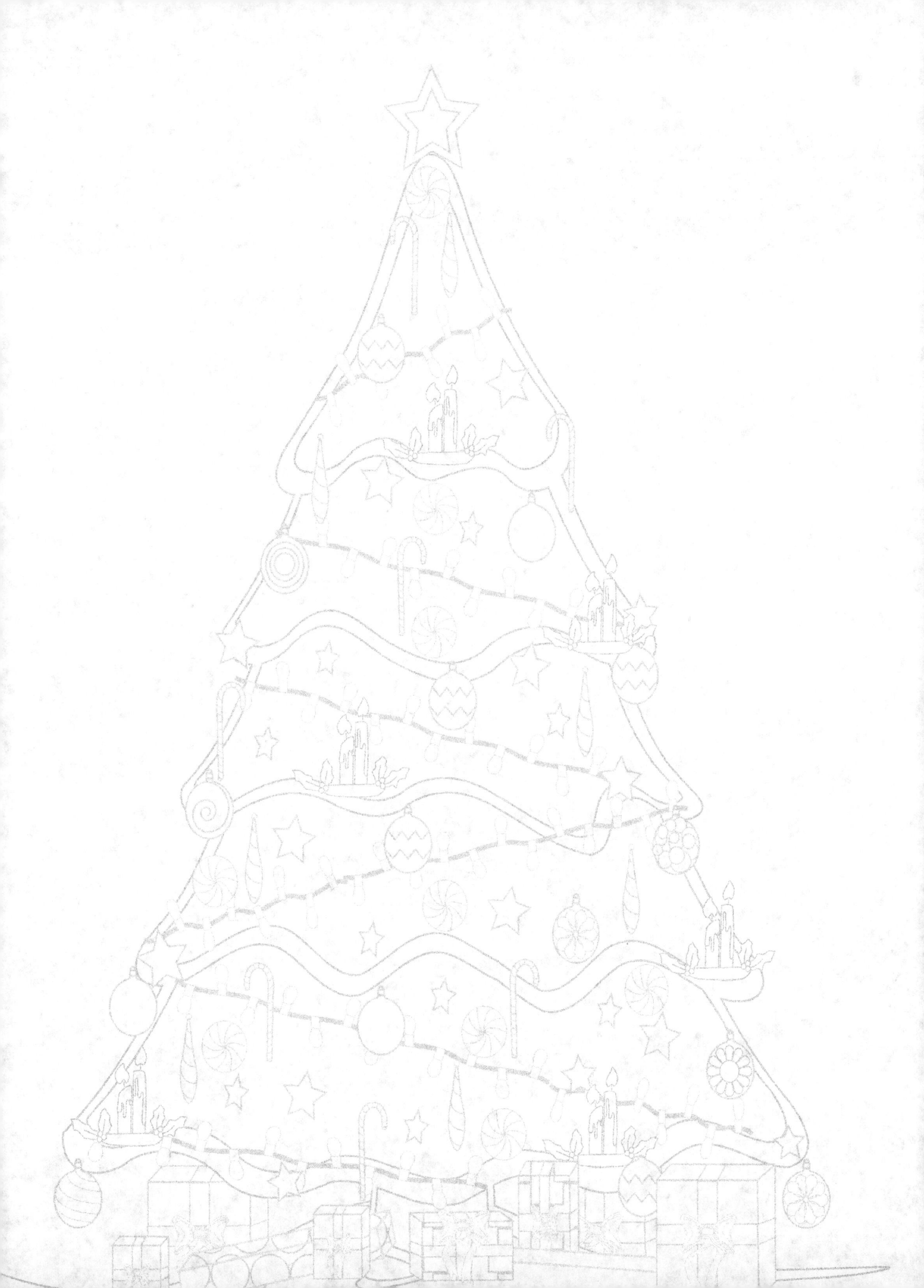

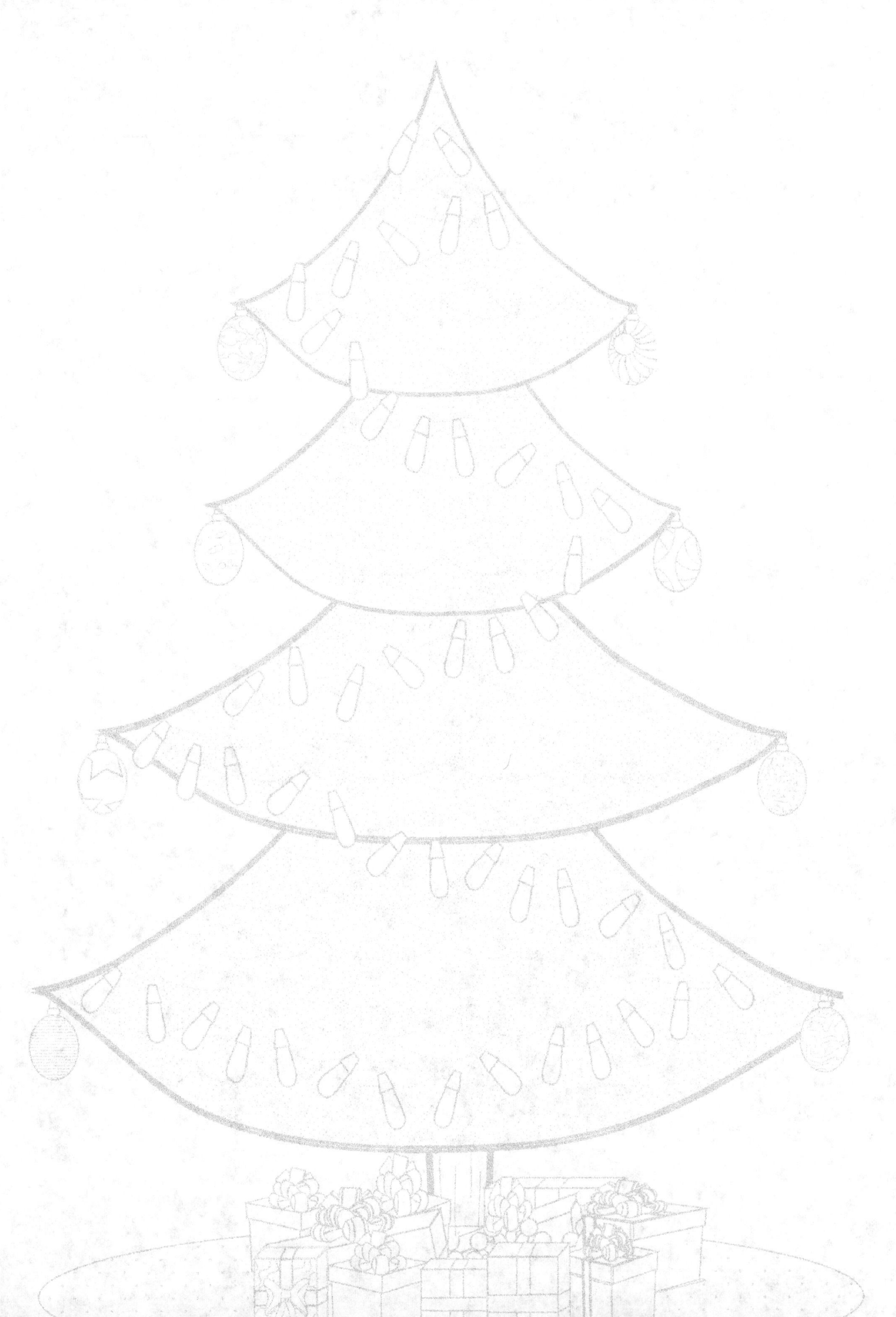

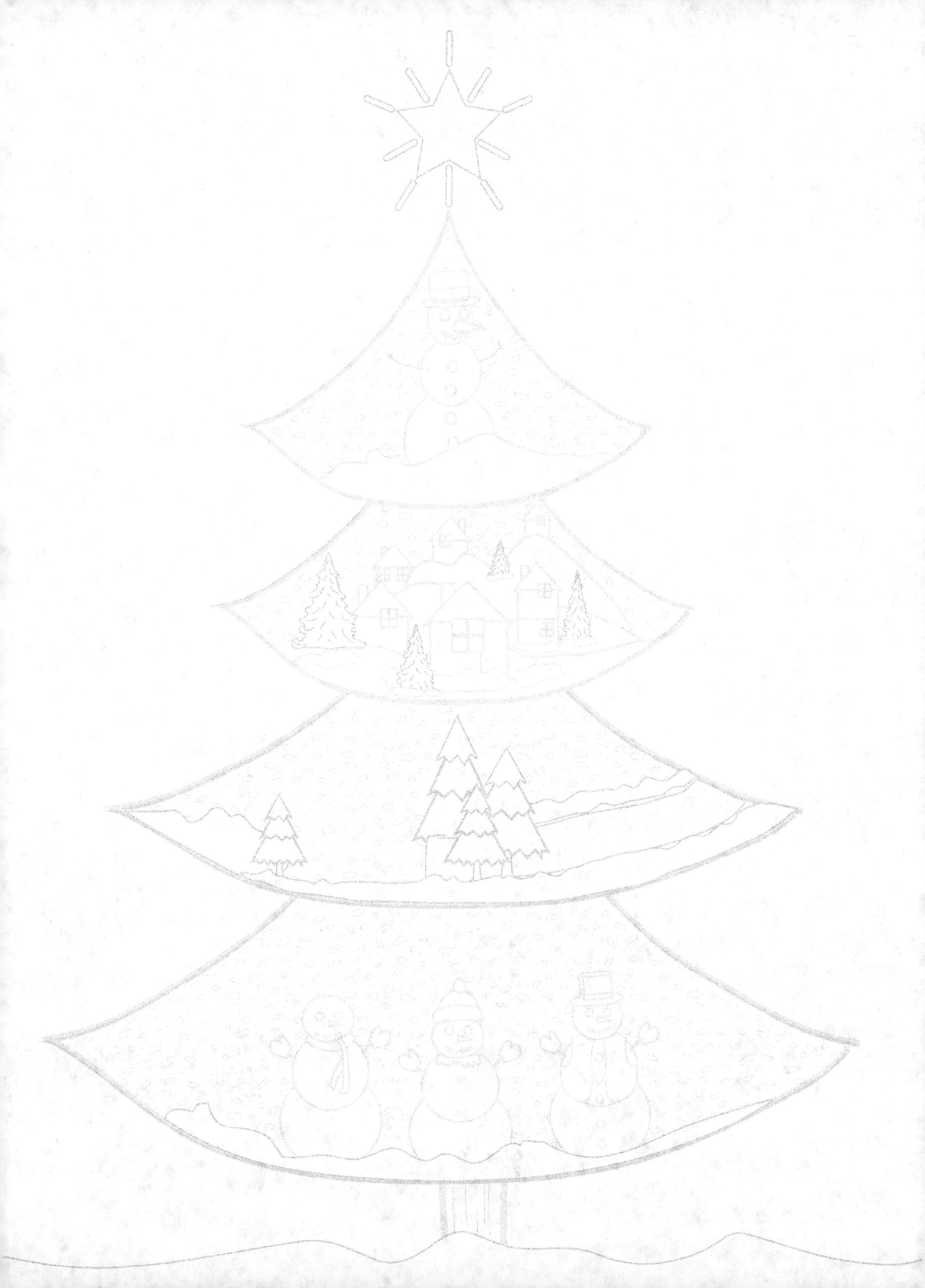

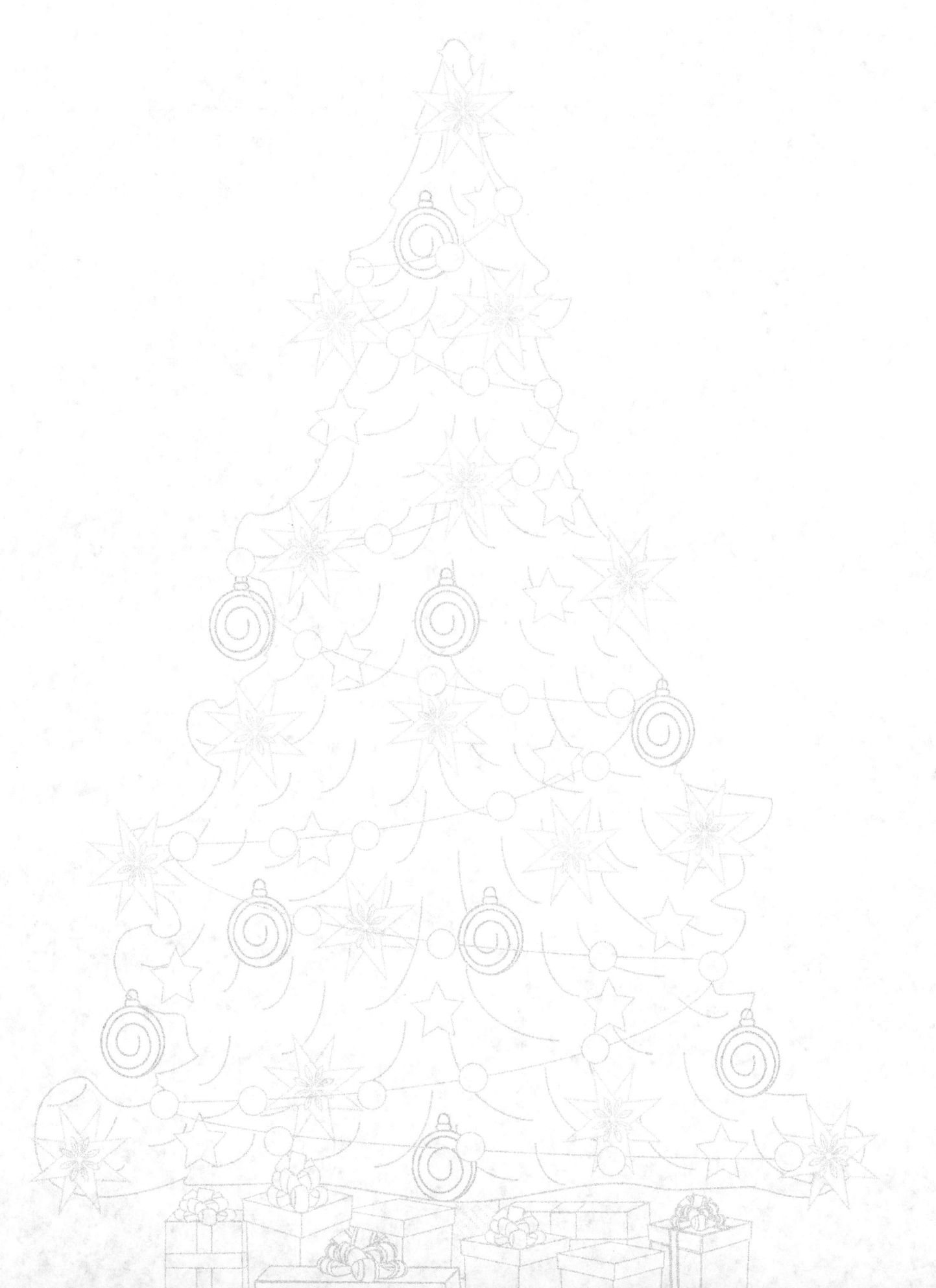

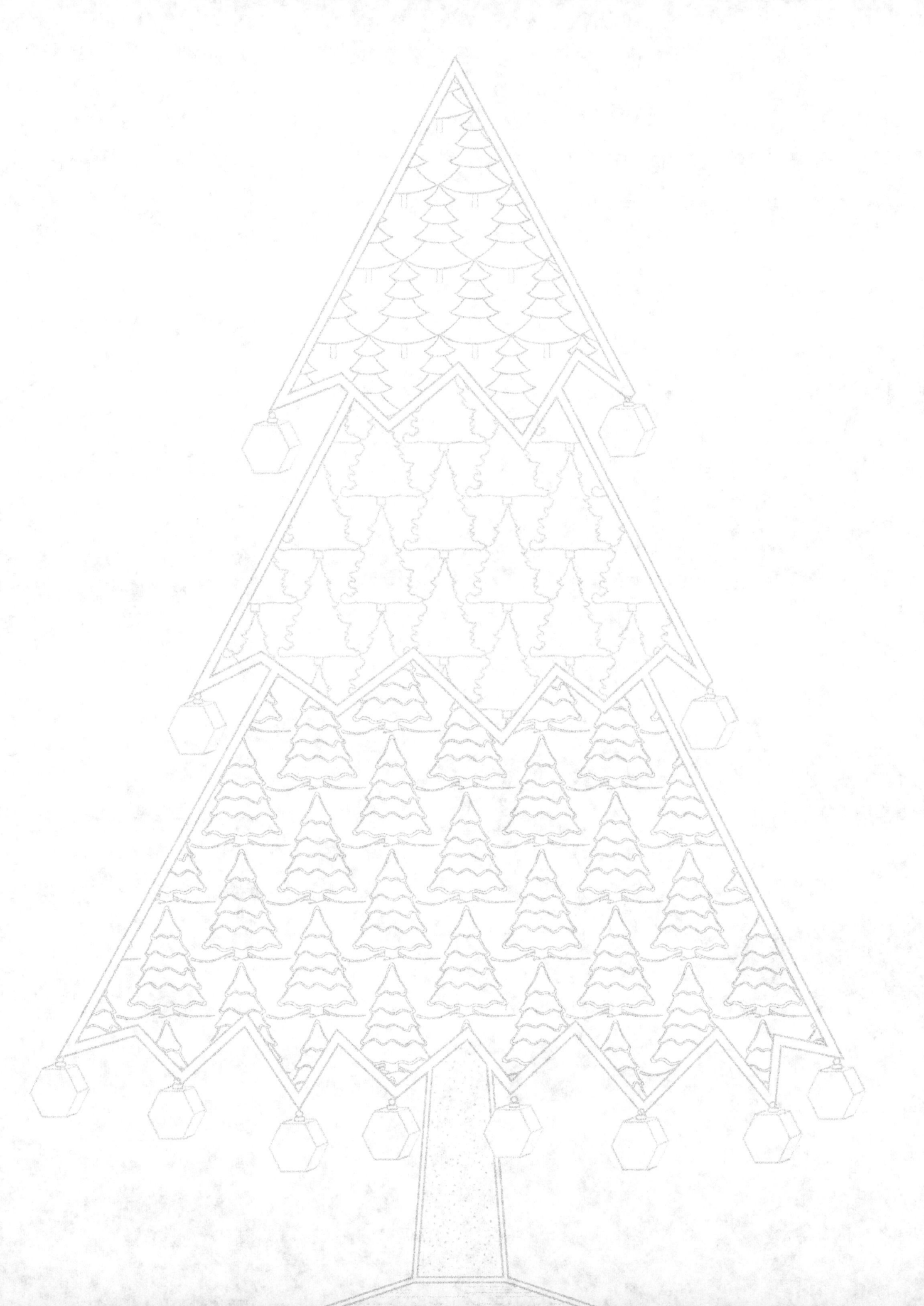

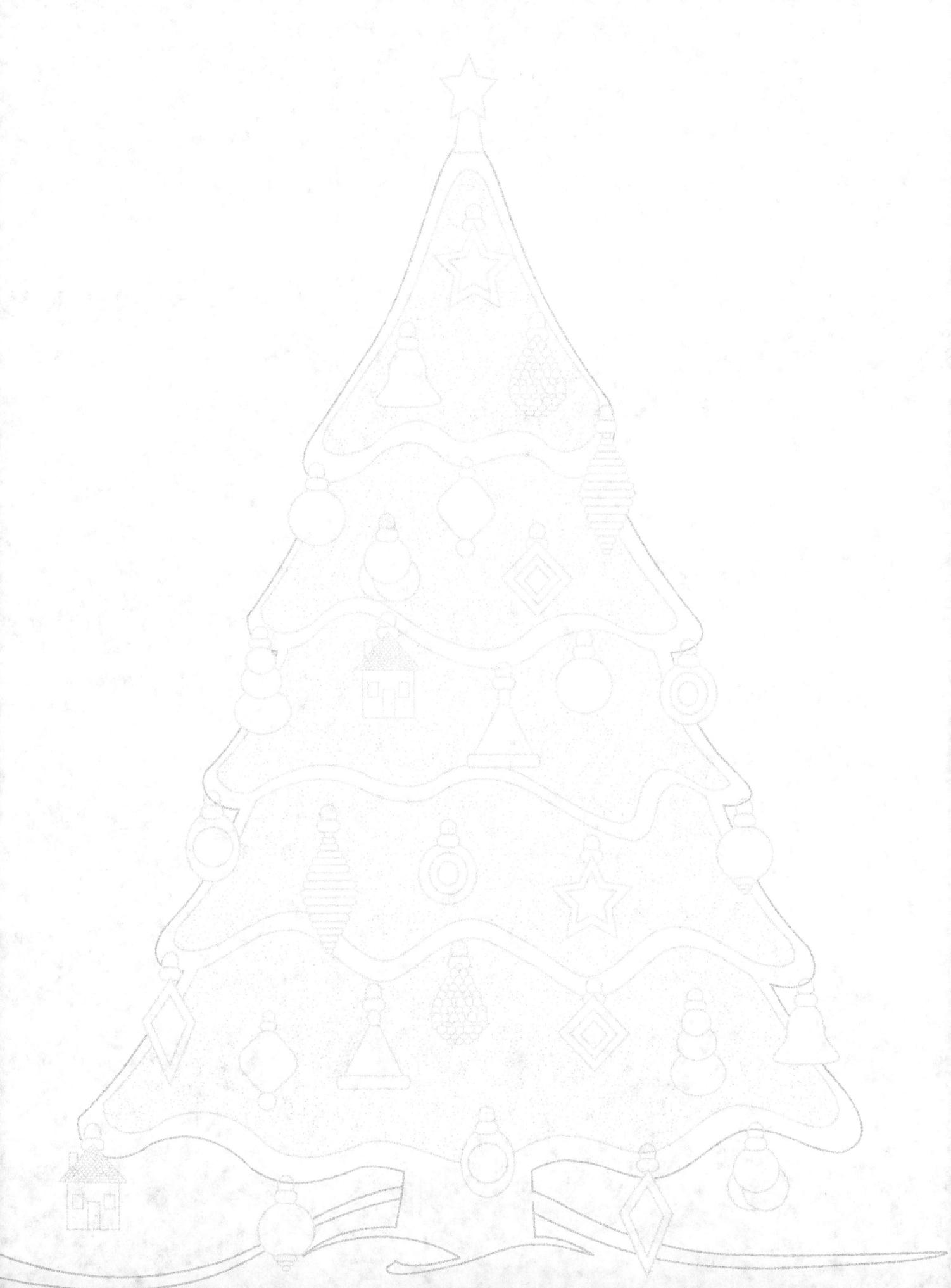

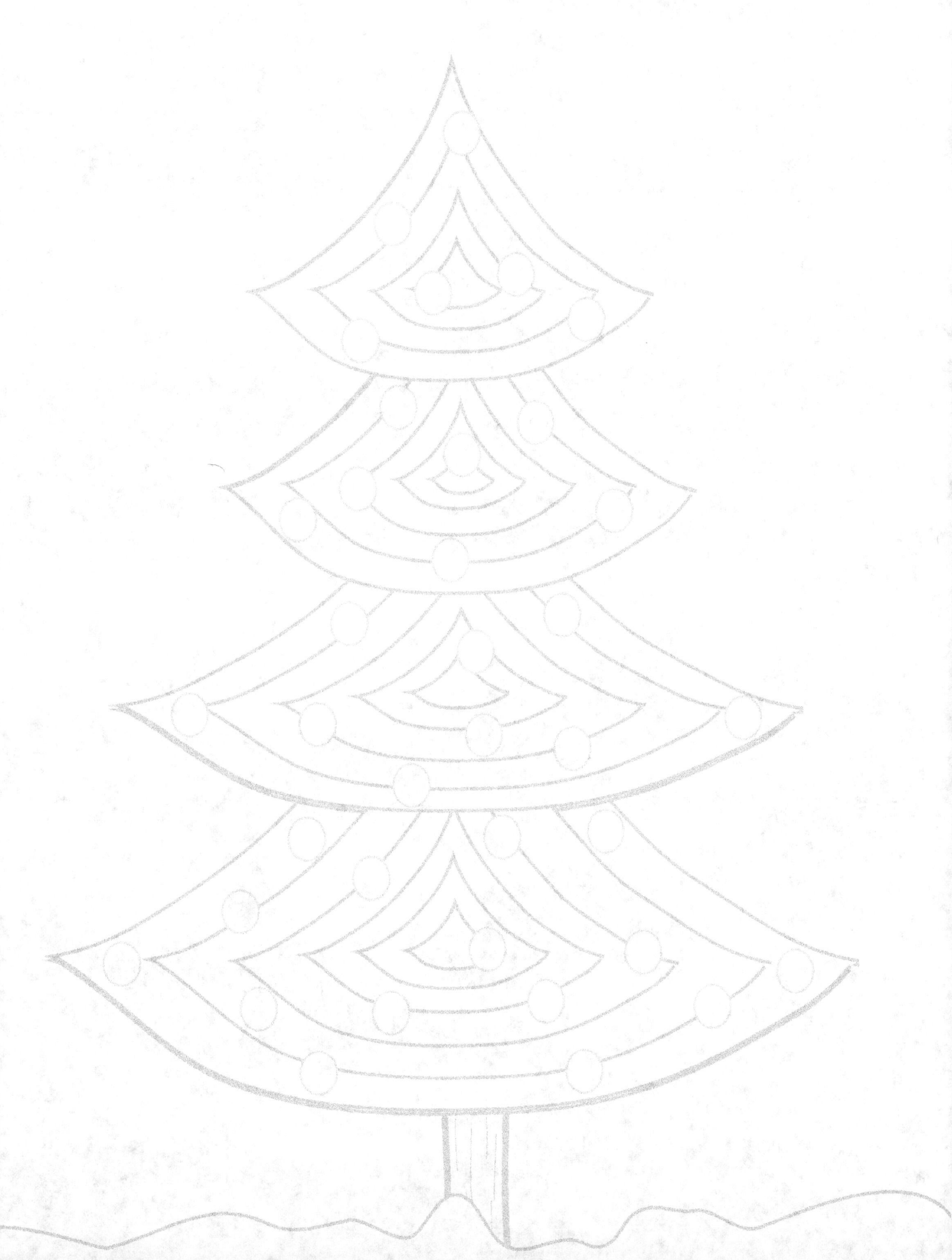

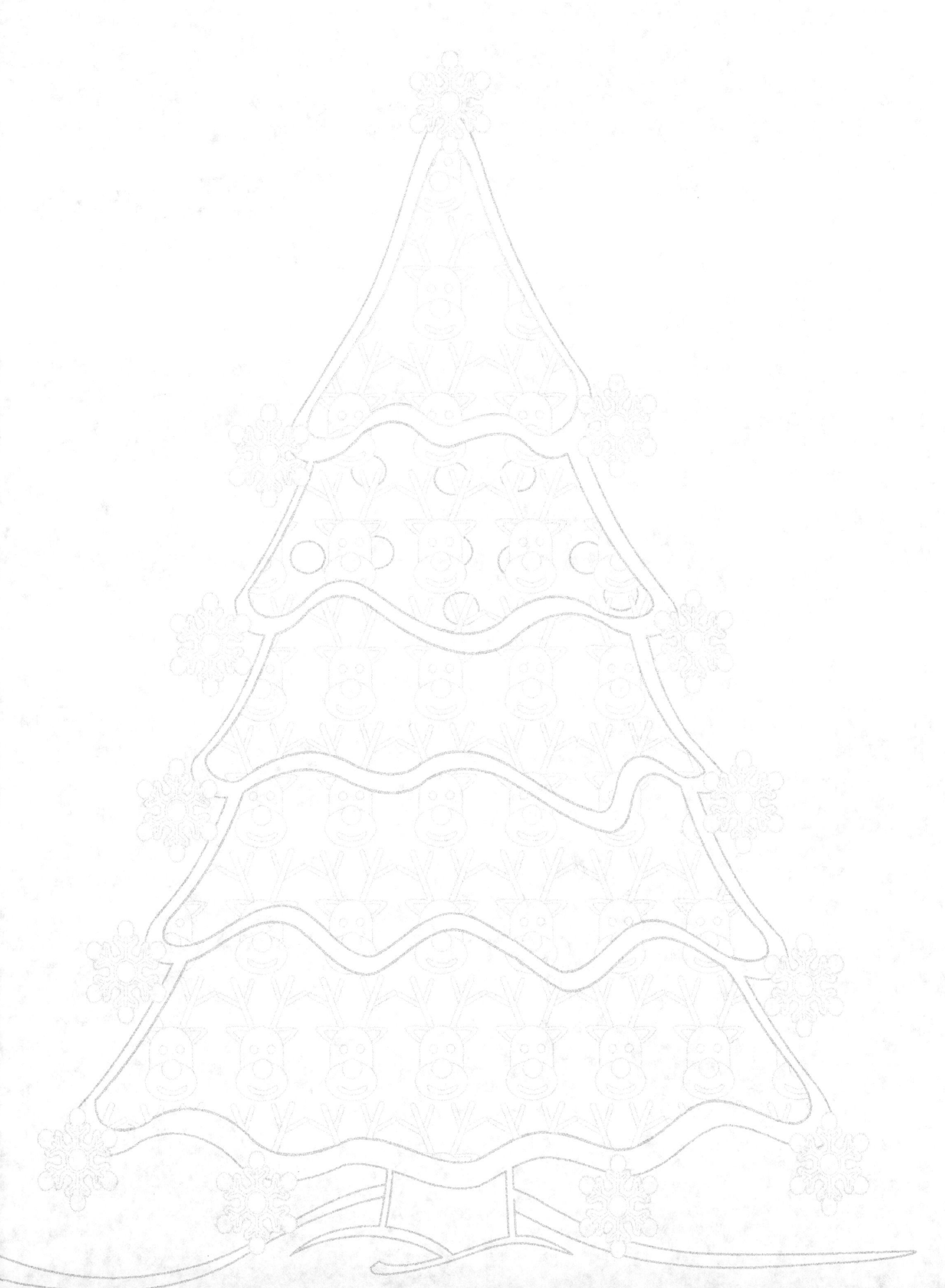

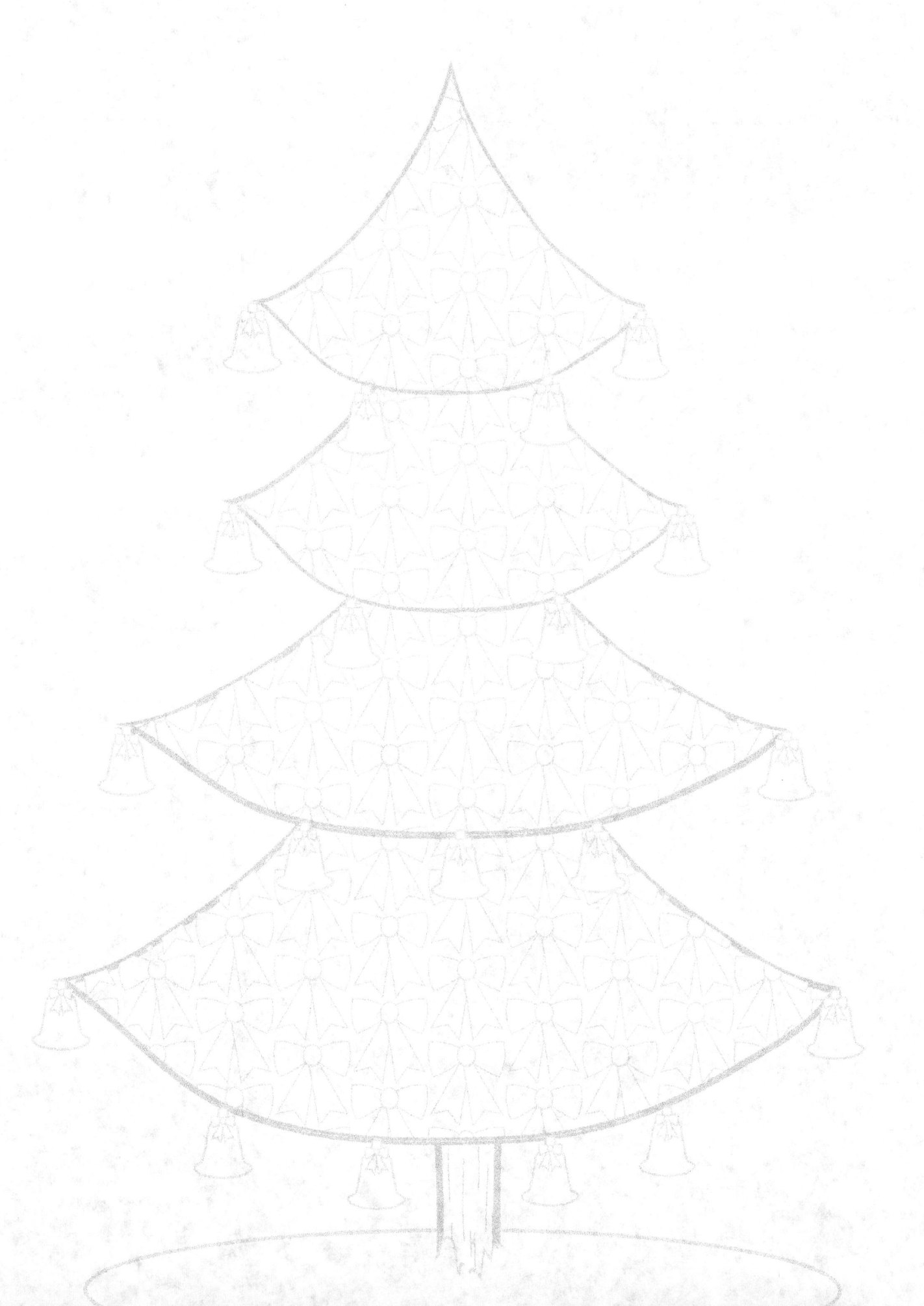

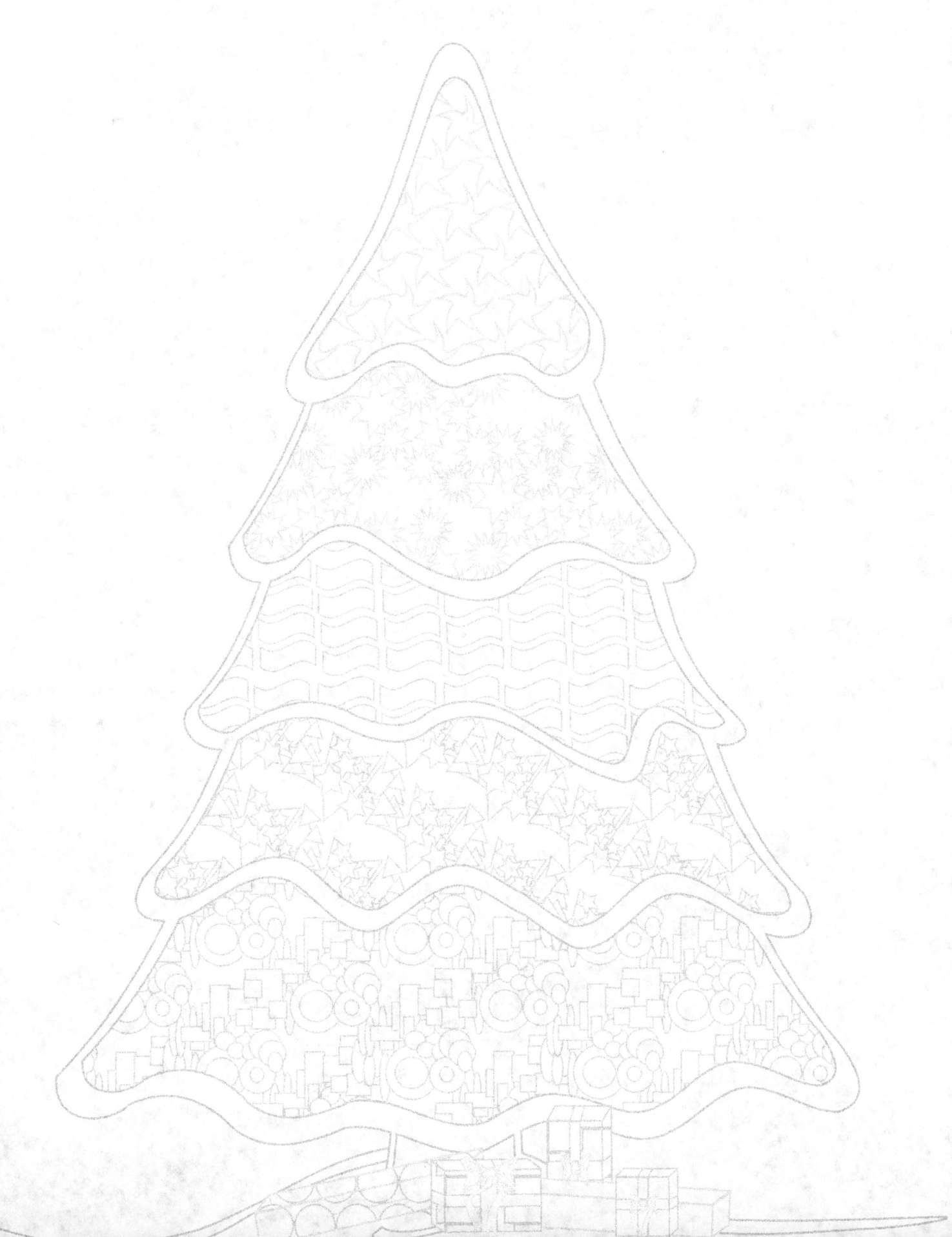

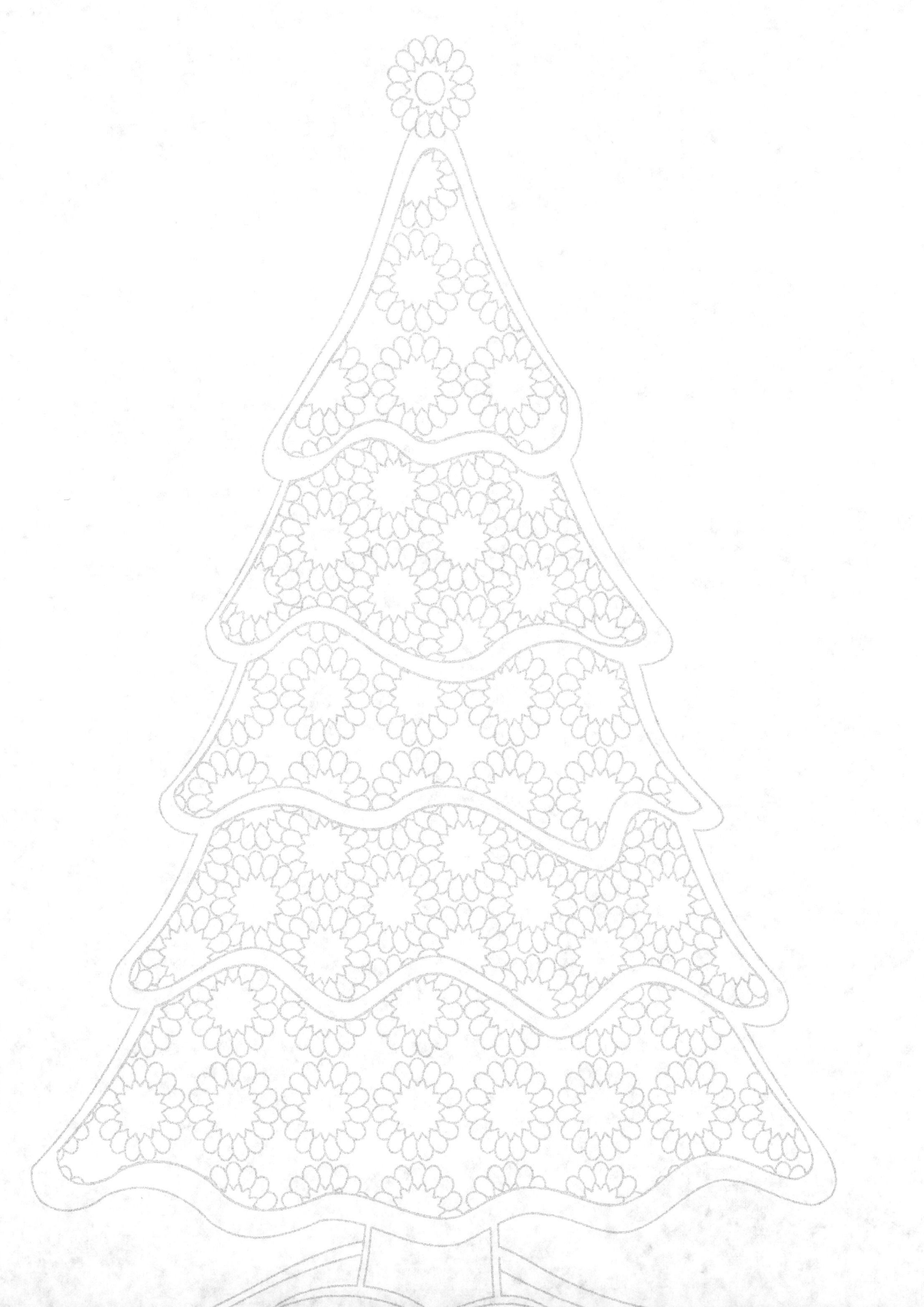

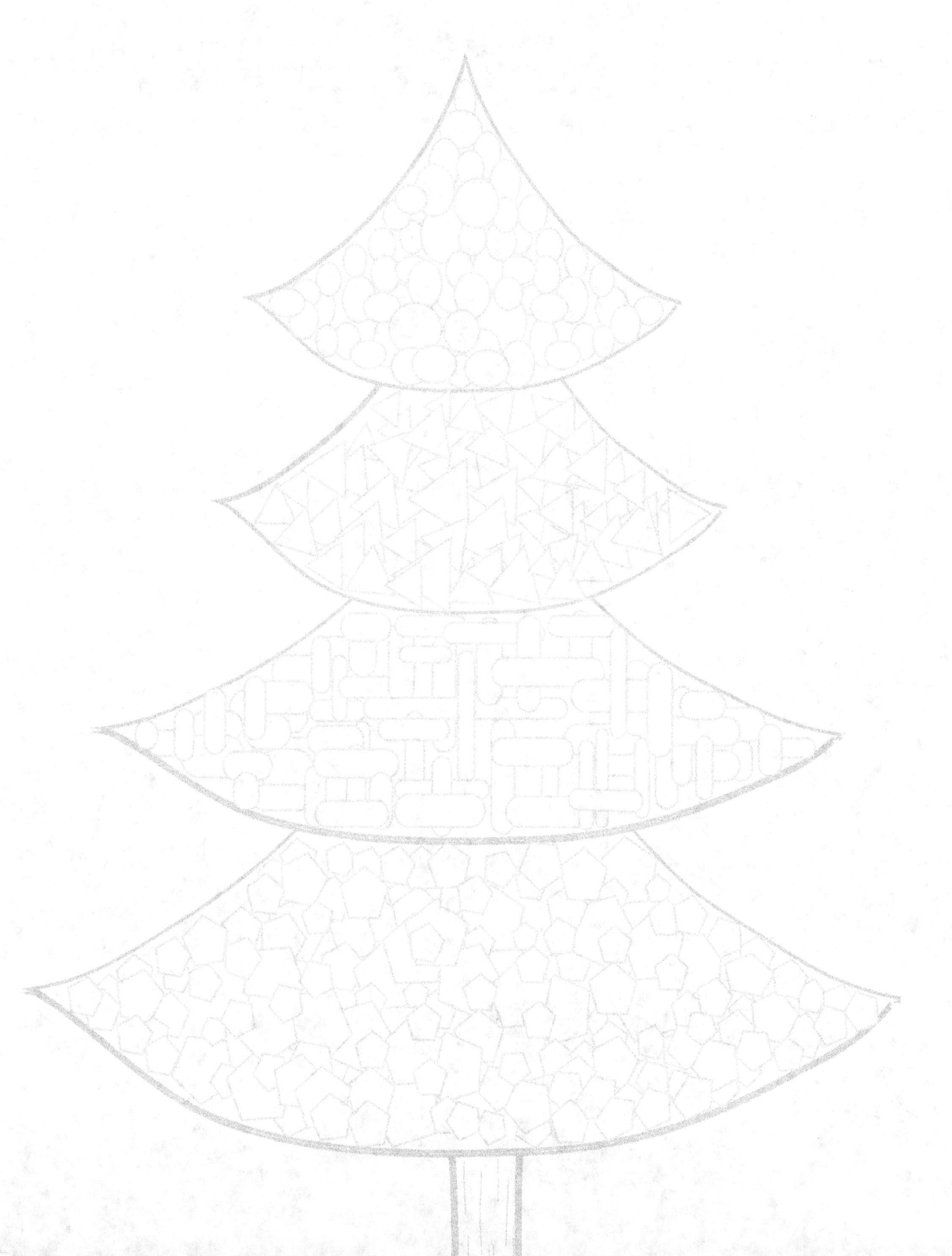

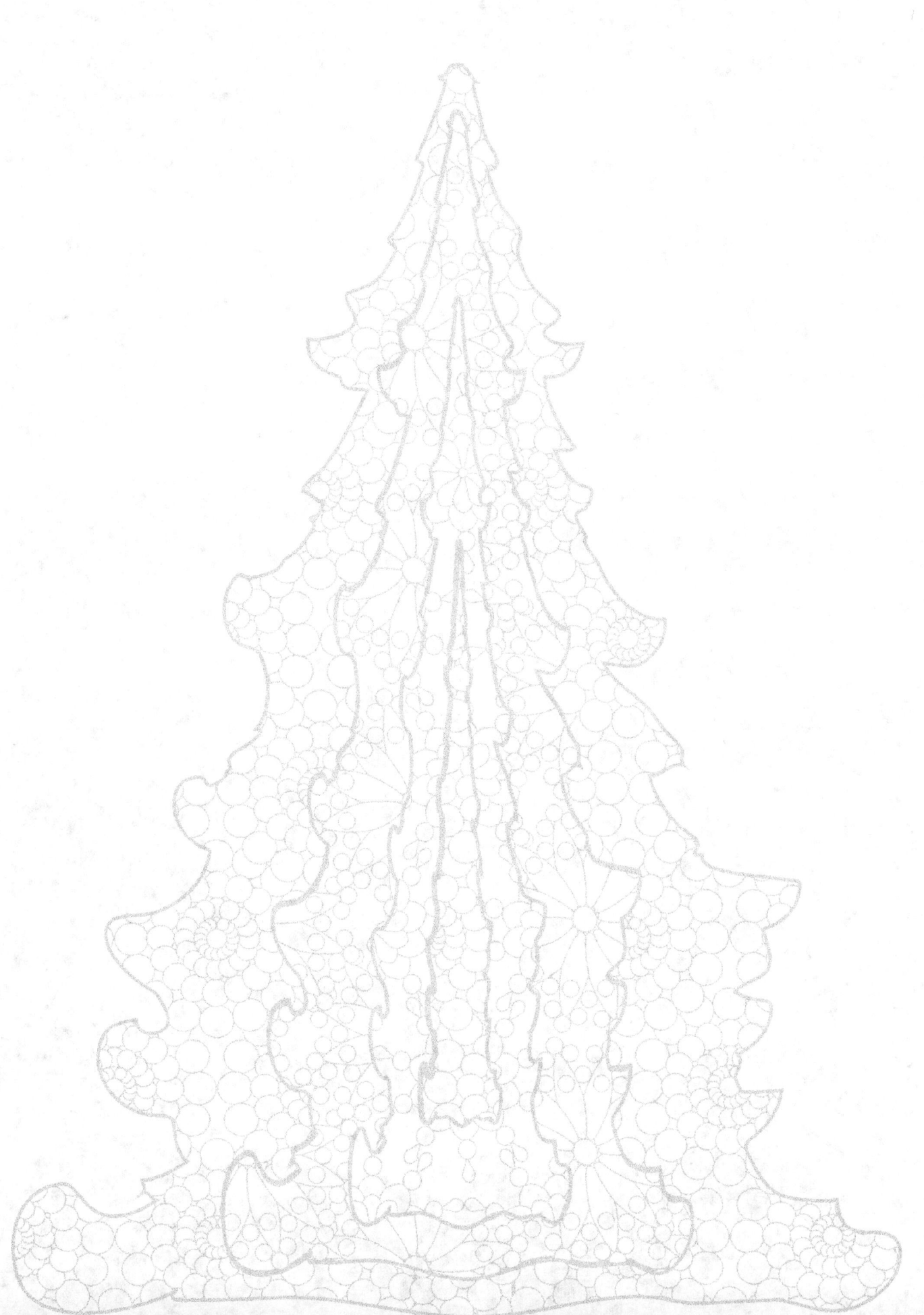

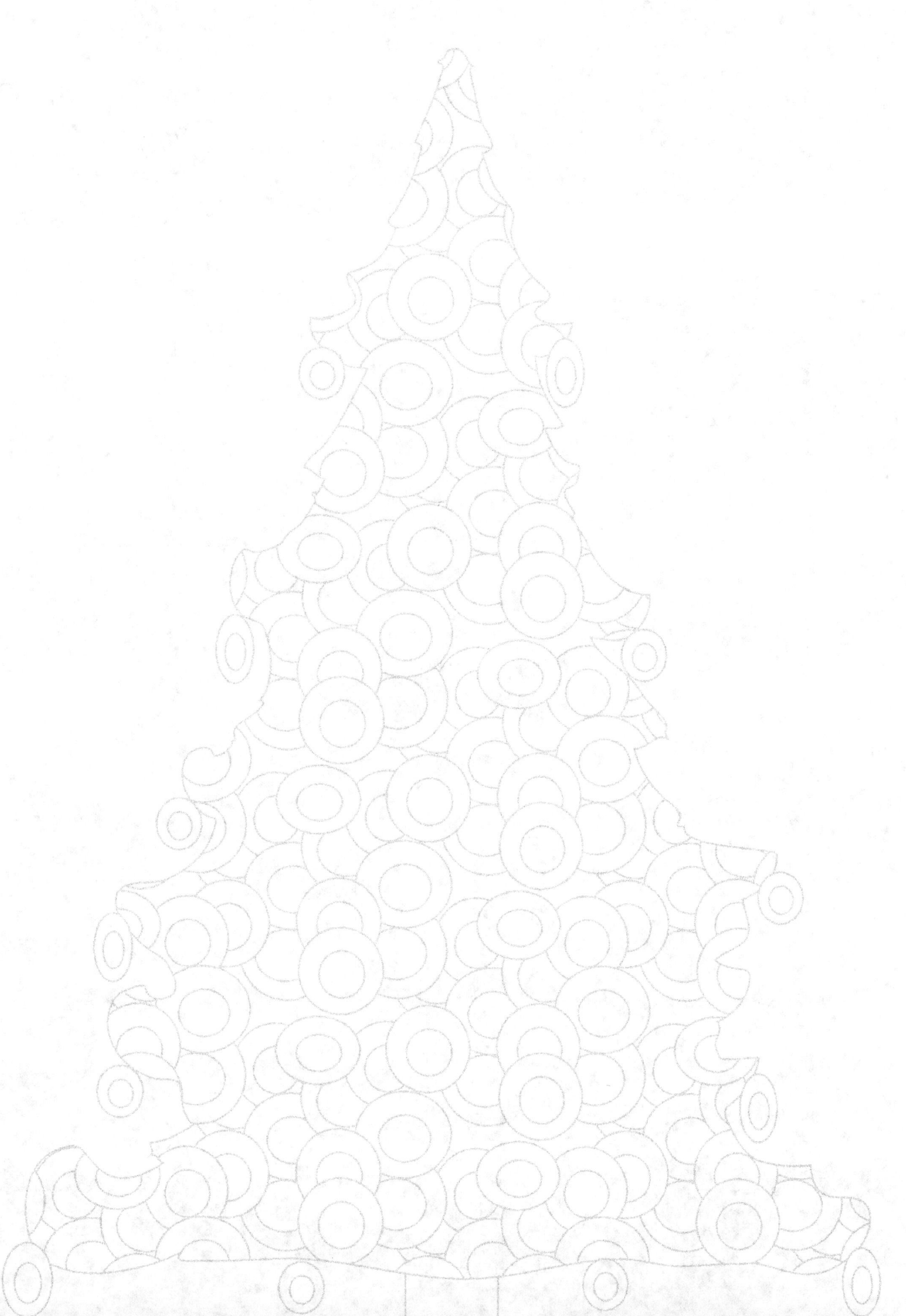

www.ingramcontent.com/pod-product-compliance
Lightning Source LLC
Chambersburg PA
CBHW081614220526
45468CB00010B/2869